THE MIZ

BY JIM BREW

BELLWETHER MEDIA · MINNEAPOLIS, MN

Are you ready to take it to the extreme?
Torque books thrust you into the action-packed world
of sports, vehicles, mystery, and adventure. These books
may include dirt, smoke, fire, and dangerous stunts.
WARNING : read at your own risk.

Library of Congress Cataloging-in-Publication Data

Brew, Jim.
The Miz / by Jim Brew.
    p. cm. -- (Torque: pro wrestling champions)
Includes bibliographical references and index.
Summary: "Engaging images accompany information about The Miz. The combination of high-interest
subject matter and light text is intended for students in grades 3 through 7"--Provided by publisher.
ISBN 978-1-60014-753-1 (hardcover : alk. paper)
1. Miz, 1980--- Juvenile literature. 2. Wrestlers--United States--Biography--Juvenile literature. I. Title.
GV1196.M59B74 2012
796.812092--dc23
[B]   2011032309

Printed in the United States of America, North Mankato, MN.

010112   1202

CONTENTS

CASHING IN

The crowd booed as The Miz rushed out to the ring at Amway Center in Orlando, Florida. World Wrestling Entertainment (WWE) Champion Randy Orton had just won a tough match against Wade Barrett. The Miz carried the briefcase he had won in a Money in the Bank **ladder match**. The case allowed him to challenge for any WWE title at any time. Orton was tired and his knee was injured. The Miz was ready to take advantage.

VITAL STATS

Wrestling Name: _____The Miz

Real Name: _____ Michael Gregory Mizanin

Height: _____6 feet, 2 inches (1.9 meters)

Weight: _____ 220 pounds (100 kilograms)

Started Wrestling: _____2003

Finishing Move: _____ Skull-Crushing Finale

The Miz went on the attack. He hammered on Orton's injured knee. Orton fought back despite a bad limp. He went for his **finishing move**, but The Miz reversed it. He wrapped his arms around Orton and slammed him face-first into the mat in his powerful **Skull-Crushing Finale**. The Miz rolled onto Orton for the pin and the victory. He had done it! WWE had a new champion!

QUICK HIT!

The Miz nicknamed himself "The Awesome One." He called his WWE Championship reign "The Era of Awesome."

WHO IS THE MIZ?

Michael Gregory Mizanin was born on October 8, 1980 in Parma, Ohio. He was a huge wrestling fan as a child. Mike was a good athlete and leader in high school. He was the captain of his basketball and cross-country teams. After high school, Mike went to Miami University of Ohio. He studied business, but he wanted to be an actor.

In 2001, MTV selected Mike to join the cast of *The Real World*. He left college and went to New York City for the show. *The Real World* features a group of young strangers living in a house together. Mike was usually calm and collected. He called himself The Miz when he got angry.

QUICK HIT!

Mike was popular with *The Real World* fans. He went on to appear in several seasons of the MTV show *Real World/ Road Rules Challenge*.

In 2003, Mike joined a small wrestling league called Ultimate Pro Wrestling (UPW). His ring name was The Miz. He earned a spot in the TV competition *Tough Enough* in 2004. Mike finished second in the competition, but WWE officials were impressed. They offered him a **developmental contract**.

BECOMING A CHAMPION

The Miz continued to work on his wrestling skills in small leagues in 2005 and 2006. He joined WWE in 2006 as a TV host. He got his first chance to wrestle in September. The Miz defeated Tatanka in his **debut**. He became a **heel** who mocked other wrestlers.

The Miz won his first singles title in 2009. He defeated Kofi Kingston to win the United States Championship. In 2010, he won a ladder match and a Money in the Bank briefcase. He used that case to challenge and defeat Randy Orton. His Era of Awesome lasted an impressive six months.

QUICK HIT!

The Miz was once banned from wrestling in several big WWE events. He wore a mask and wrestled as The Calgary Kid so he could get in the ring.

DISCUS PUNCH

The Miz's skills and **showmanship** have made him a WWE success. Fans know him for his **signature moves**. For the Discus Punch, he spins around to build up a powerful punch. He also uses the Swinging Corner Clothesline. The Miz gets his opponent into a corner of the ring. Then he charges and slams his arm into the opponent's neck.

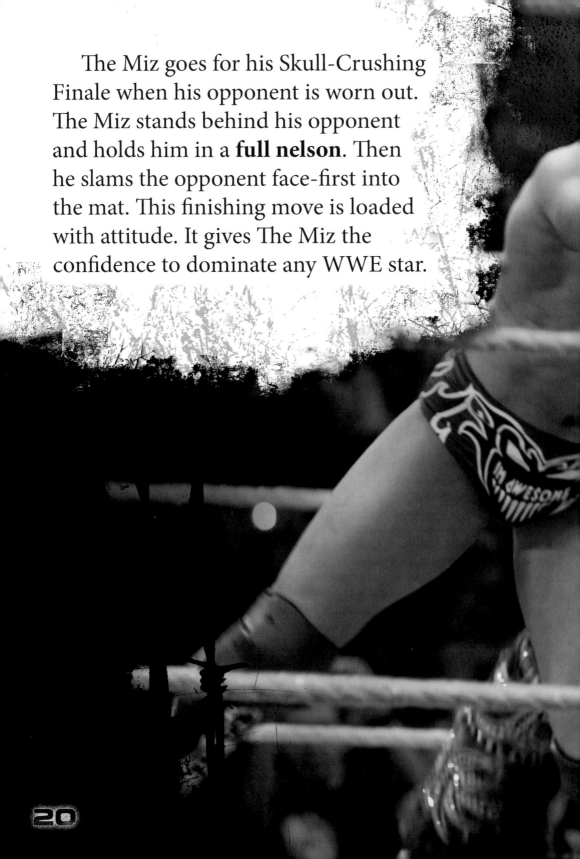

The Miz goes for his Skull-Crushing Finale when his opponent is worn out. The Miz stands behind his opponent and holds him in a **full nelson**. Then he slams the opponent face-first into the mat. This finishing move is loaded with attitude. It gives The Miz the confidence to dominate any WWE star.

SKULL-
CRUSHING
FINALE

21

GLOSSARY

debut—a wrestler's first match with a wrestling league

developmental contract—an agreement in which a wrestler signs with WWE but then wrestles in a smaller league to gain experience and develop skills

finishing move—a wrestling move meant to finish off an opponent so that he can be pinned

full nelson—a wrestling move in which one wrestler holds another from behind; he wraps his arms under the opponent's shoulders and locks his fingers behind the opponent's neck.

heel—a wrestler seen by fans as a villain

ladder match—a wrestling match in which a ladder is placed in the middle of the ring; the first wrestler to reach the object at the top wins the match.

showmanship—the ability to do something in an exciting or engaging manner

signature moves—moves that a wrestler is famous for performing

Skull-Crushing Finale—The Miz's finishing move; The Miz holds an opponent in a full nelson, then slams him face-first into the mat.

TO LEARN MORE

AT THE LIBRARY

Black, Jake. *The Ultimate Guide to WWE*. New York, N.Y.: Grosset & Dunlap, 2010.

Kaelberer, Angie Peterson. *Cool Pro Wrestling Facts*. Mankato, Minn.: Capstone Press, 2011.

Stone, Adam. *Randy Orton*. Minneapolis, Minn.: Bellwether Media, Inc., 2012.

ON THE WEB

Learning more about The Miz is as easy as 1, 2, 3.

1. Go to www.factsurfer.com.

2. Enter "The Miz" into the search box.

3. Click the "Surf" button and you will see a list of related Web sites.

With factsurfer.com, finding more information is just a click away.

INDEX

The images in this book are reproduced through the courtesy of: Moses Robinson / Getty Images, front cover, p. 14; Rick Scuteri / Associated Press, p. 4; Devin Chen, pp. 5, 7, 10-11, 12-13, 20-21; Jordan Strauss / Getty Images, pp. 8-9; John Smolek, pp. 15, 16-17; Paul Abell / Associated Press, pp. 18-19.